©2002 Studio Mouse, and the Smithsonian Institution, Washington, D.C. 20560 USA.

Published by McGraw-Hill Children's Publishing, a Division of The McGraw-Hill Companies.

ll inquiries to:
-Hill Children's Publishing • 8787 Orion Place • Columbus, Ohio 43240

845-465-7

7 8 9 10 CHRT 08 07 06 05 04 03 02 01

na.

nks to Dr. Beth B. Norden of the Department of Entomology at the Smithsonian
um of Natural History for her curatorial review.

The Busy Bumblebee

... of ...
stor...
Send ...
McGra...
ISBN 1-5...
1 2 3 4 5 6
Printed in Ch...

Acknowledgements
Our very special tha...
Institution's National Mu...

WOODLAND MIL...

The Busy Bumblebee

by Laura Gates Galvin   Illustrated by Kristin Kest

McGraw-Hill
Children's Publishing

In the bright sunshine of early spring, a fuzzy black-and-yellow bumblebee crawls out of the ground after a long winter's nap.

Bumblebee's body is cool from the ground. She vibrates her flight muscles to warm herself before buzzing her way to a patch of clover for a sip of nectar.

Bumblebee begins searching for a
homesite, and finds an abandoned
field mouse's nest in the hollow
of a birch tree that is just right.

Bumblebee carefully clears all of the sticks and dirt from her new nest, then shapes a tiny honey pot out of her own wax, before visiting more spring blossoms.

Returning to the nest, Bumblebee fills the honey pot with nectar she has collected in her stomach, then lays eight eggs into another wax pot, and settles on top to keep them warm.

When Bumblebee's eggs hatch into larvae, she busily collects pollen, placing it in small pockets on the sides of the wax pot for the larvae to eat.

After a week, Bumblebee's well-fed larvae spin themselves into separate tiny cocoons. Bumblebee makes more wax pots beside the cocoons and lays more eggs.

When two weeks have passed,
Bumblebee helps her daughters,
eight silvery-gray worker bees,
out of their silken cocoons.

19

Bumblebee's daughters are good workers, helping her to feed the next group of larvae and clean the nest. Bumblebee, the queen bee, stays busy laying more eggs.

In the hot, humid days of August, the nest becomes a flurry of activity. Three bees hover at the top of the nest, fluttering their wings to keep their home cool.

Worker bees buzz from flowers to honey pots, collecting pollen and nectar for Bumblebee to sip while she continues to lay eggs.

Suddenly, a carpenter ant enters the nest. A worker bee flips on her back, opens her jaws, and points her stinger in warning at the ant, frightening him away.

October arrives in a burst of red, orange, and yellow. Bumblebee's last eggs have hatched, producing new queens and males.

The worker bees will die as the air gets cold. The young queens will hibernate underground in the winter, each waking in the spring to begin her own new colony.

About the Bumblebee

There are at least 300 different species of bumblebee found throughout the world, except in arctic regions, and life cycles vary from species to species and climate to climate. Bumblebees can lay six to ten eggs at one time, producing young, pale-colored bees with soft fur and matted wings. Soon, their bodies harden, turning vibrant shades of yellow and black, orange and white—even shades of red. Most wildflowers and cultivated crops depend on bumblebees for their unique methods of pollination, including "buzz pollination" in which the vibration from a bee's flight muscles shake the tightly packed pollen out of the flower.